*Elevate Your Greatness 50 and Beyond*

# ROCK YOUR 50 PLUS

*The Secret Diary for Women 50 and Beyond*

## MS. DIAMOND

# Inspiring You to Rock YOUR Greatness
## While looking and Feeling Fabulous!!

I am a Certified Life and Health Coach. I empower women and help re-create lives of women 50 and beyond to be sexy, vibrant, energized pivoting their dreams and goals.

Being way over 50 myself, I decided to change my lifestyle and start living a healthier and greater me. Most people don't believe my age, however it comes from years of studying different cultures during my overseas travels as an entertainer. It encouraged me to change my way of life and create a life with more love, better health, an abundance of wisdom and prosperity.

I was an orphan at the age 5 growing up in Flint, Michigan. I went from foster home to foster home until a family decided to adopt me and my younger brother. Although it was a better life than where I came from, it was very difficult for me as a child to adapt to the rules and religious pressures of my adopted family. It was so dysfunctional that at age 13, I left my adopted family. I turned myself in to the system refusing to go back to their home. Which lead me back to foster home after foster home. This lead to continuous hard times going forward for quite a few years.

Drug abuse, domestic violence, self-hatred and more. It was ruthless returning back to foster home after foster home. For decades

I was oblivious as to where I was going, I had no direction. Lost in a cold and crazy unloving world.

At age 25 things started to turn around. I had the opportunity to go overseas with my beautiful husband and our show band, with me as the lead vocalist. I had never been outside of the US. However, I took a chance and made that dramatic change to go and perform overseas.

Back when I was in my early 20's, my friend and I at the time use to dream of being in the music business. We would imagine ourselves wealthy in the entertainment world even though we were caught up in a dangerous world of drugs and low self-esteem at the time. During that time, we created stage names for each other. I named her London because she always wanted to go to London and she named me Diamond because of my love for diamonds. Diamonds can go from being in the rough unpolished to sparkle and shine as bright as the sun. That's when my stage name Diamond was born.

Finally, I entered my journey of being in the music world as a lead vocalist. I utilized my stage name Ms. Diamond, while traveling overseas from one country to the another. I grew and became a professional entertainer, within leaving the US on a 3 month contract. Leaving on my contract turned into over 20 years of an amazing life with exciting experiences, more financial freedom and being an entrepreneur.

That was also the beginning of my health and wellness journey to changing my lifestyle. I learned many different cultures and their healthier way of life. Japan being the biggest and the most influential. I implemented a whole new way of life and eating habits that lead me to where I am now.

Also, being an entertainer, I wanted to look good and feel good, so that my performances would have a great impact on the audience. I became one of the most requested singers in Southeast Asia. Performing on stage with some of the greatest performers ever. I also shared the same stage with Michael Jackson Tokyo VIP Event, Mariah Carey Japanese TV Debut and John Legend, just to name a few.

When I returned back to the US after being in the 2011 three natural disasters in Tokyo, I landed a 9 to 5, not my cup of tea and it was during a depression. Jobs weren't plentiful like they were when I left. After going through a few jobs, I landed a great job in the trade show business with a good company.

During that time, I faced another diversity in my life. The day my husband and I separated. I had been with my husband for 30 years at that time. It was very devastating. Also, my daughter had left without us knowing. She left to live her life on her own in another state.

Going through so much inner turmoil, that was also a turning point in my life. It was at that moment I realized I wanted to be able to help women. I wanted to help women like myself be able to rise above standards. Not just be known for being a wife, mother and helping everyone else except themselves. I didn't want them to forget their own dreams and goals.

I decided to go to school and become a Life and Health Coach, which took my mind off being separated from my husband. I began to put the pieces together for my own life and what I desired and what I wanted out of life. I didn't realize how much I had become so dependent on my husband, that I lost myself in the process.

My husband and I worked out our marriage and it has become better the second time around. I believe it is because I began living for me! It took some time to get to this place. Life is about growth and learning how to be a better and greater you.

That is why I wrote this book. I know I am not the only woman who has experienced trauma in their life, that will create a massive change to better themselves. I now live my life exploring and growing into the woman I desire to be. Living on my own terms following the path God has laid out for me. Everyday I'm a work in progress to always be self-supporting towards my dreams and goals, unstoppable and non-negotiable.

I hope you enjoy this book and it helps you as much as it has helped me in becoming the woman I desire.

It is my hope to give you encouragement with accountability to accomplish your dreams and goals, turning them into your reality. When you implement the tools within this book you will gain self-confidence, beauty, inner peace, self-joy, bravery, and all the above.

Here is my toast to you and your fearless journey!

I Would Like To Give Thanks To God!

My Loved Ones, Family And Friends For Believing In Me
And Never Giving Up On Me!

I Love You To The Moon And Back!

# Contents

# Contents

# Introduction

I am writing this book in hope to inspire women over 50 globally to live their "Greater Living After 50". If you have lived your whole adult life taking care of others, this book is for you. There comes a time in a woman's life that she must take into consideration her needs and wants before anyone else. I know a lot of us do not know how to do this after dedicating our entire being to others and putting ourselves on the back end of life.

Not anymore, this book is the beginning of a new start, a new extraordinary you. It's time to get busy taking charge of your life wants, desires and all the above.

This is your time.

*"You don't have to be great to start but you have to start to be great"*
~ Zig Ziglar

www.greaterlivingafter50.com
Facebook: greaterlivingafter50
Instagram: iamcoachpauladiamond
Youtube: greaterlivingafter50
Email: info@greaterlivingafter50.com

# Let's Do It

I know you have thought to yourself how am I going to accomplish my desires and dreams. Well, someone once told me don't worry about the how, put in the work, focus, ask for spiritual guidance and never give up.

Let's do it by looking inside ourselves. When you look inside yourself you must be willing to go deep within and ask yourself these questions:

## Take Action Challenge

1. What do I want to achieve?

_____

2. What do I have to offer that will make it a reality?

_____

3. Are you willing to put in the work to make it happen?

_____

4. Do you have the discipline to keep going even when times are difficult?

_____

5. What are your gifts?

_____

If you were able to answer these questions honestly, I encourage you to keep going and know that all things are working out for your good and faithful work.

However, if you were not able to answer the following questions, I encourage you to look deeper inside yourself and proceed to find your inner ability to answer the questions. Once you are able to answer, you will then begin to have a clearer perspective on your purpose.

Take time out everyday to reflect on the questions and start your journey living your purpose. We all have a purpose and we all have dreams. Some of us need help and tools to begin reaching inside ourselves to start putting it all together.

Even though we don't have all the answers and the how, what we do have is ourselves and our spiritual guidance, whomever that may be for you.

Get focused and commit to yourself with a written out plan. You also need persistence, to not deter from your direct plan or your purpose to reach your goal.

If you need to hire a coach for accountability do so! Whatever you do, "Let's Do It" by staying determined, disciplined and dedicated to your purpose and dreams.

# Notes

# Notes

# Finding The Lost You

Somehow in the process of taking care of everybody else but you, somewhere along the way you lost yourself. You lost who you are, your dreams, your goals along with your desires. In the course of searching for ones self, we begin to look for outside validation. You feel as though something is missing from your life and you just don't know quite what it is. With the hustle and bustle of your daily life with work, family, etc. you're trying to find your sense of purpose.

Well, let me enlighten you with the thought of, you just might be missing you. With all that's going on in the world today we are continuously pulled from all directions, which takes us further and further away from ourselves. Our lives are steady in motion moving faster and faster with social media, work, family, going here, going there. No wonder most people feel off course as though they are not living their purpose.

I encourage you to get still and take an inner journey within you. Start reflecting on yourself and your development as to who you desire to be and live, from this point on. The more connected you are and centered with what you want out of life, the closer you'll get to finding the lost you.

I would like to provide you with a few helpful tips that will guide you in finding the lost you.

**Helpful Tips**

1.  Start your day with a morning practice such as gratitude and prayer.

2.  Start journaling, this will help you re-establish a relationship with you.

3.  Write down your dreams, desires and goals.

4.  Become apart of a community, some type of support group. Being around likeminded people will bring a sense of comfort.

5.  Get in touch with your spirituality.

6.  Think about what you enjoyed as a child and reunite yourself with that experience.

7.  Dance to your favorite song, sing, even if you can't sing, listen to your favorite music, enjoy the outdoors, take a walk etc., use your imagination as to where you would like to be 5 years from now.

8.  Do something good for yourself and don't feel guilty.

9.  Start implementing a commitment towards your goals.

10. Write out a daily or weekly plan and act on it.

Being a coach myself, I realize that some people may need assistance with accountability. If this is you, take that step and get the push you need to make your dreams become your reality.

Be strong and never lose your faith.

Faith without work is dead!

*"Don't Fake It, Firm Faith It Until You Make It"*

~ Ms. Diamond

Remember "You Define You"

*"You gain strength, courage and confidence by every experience in which you really stop to look fear in the face. You must do the thing you think you cannot do."*

~ Eleanor Roosevelt

## Write Down:

The things that are true to you already:

_____

_____

_____

_____

The things that you will make true to you now:

_____

_____

_____

_____

# Notes

# Notes

# Gratitude

Continue being thankful, appreciative and have readiness to show appreciation for your God given blessings, he will bless you even more. Remember the little things as well as you count your blessings because as I always say "it can be worse" However, the first thing I encourage you to do as soon as you rise is to give thanks for another day and give thanks for you being able to have another chance at life's purpose.

Gratitude helps people feel more positive, which is a great way to start your day! It helps with emotions, relish good experiences, improve health, deal with adversities and build resilient relationships.

*As the good book says: "This is the day which the Lord hath made; we will rejoice and be glad in it."*

*"In everything give thanks: for this is the will of God in Christ Jesus concerning you."*

*"Every good gift and every perfect gift is from above and cometh down from the Father of lights, with whom is no variableness, neither shadow of turning."*

*"And let the peace of God rule in your hearts, to the which also ye are called in one body; and be ye thankful."*

Just to name a few no matter what your belief is:

Gratitude can change your life because it makes you appreciate what you have, rather than what you don't have. It is a constant state of being.

## Gratitude Affirmation

I AM GRATEFUL FOR ANOTHER DAY

I AM GRATEFUL FOR THE AIR I BREATHE I AM GRATEFUL FOR THE LITTLE THINGS I AM GRATEFUL FOR FAMILY AND FRIENDS

I AM GRATEFUL FOR LOVING RELATIONSHIPS I AM GRATEFUL FOR LIFE LEARNINGS THAT HAVE MADE ME A BETTER PERSON I AM GRATEFUL FOR THE OPPORTUNITY TO CREATE CHANGE THAT WILL ALLOW ME TO LIVE A LIFE FULL OF COMPASSION, LOVE, KINDNESS, UNDERSTANDING AND SO MUCH MORE....

I AM GRATEFUL FOR ALL BLESSINGS

I AM GRATEFUL FOR THE VISION THAT POINTS TO WHERE I AM GOING

I AM GRATEFUL FOR A CHANCE TO LIVE MY DREAMS, PURPOSE AS WELL AS MY GOALS

I AM GRATEFUL FOR THE STRENGTH AND ABILITY TO LIVE A LIFE FULL OF ABUNDANCE, JOY, HEALTH AND WEALTH

I AM GRATEFUL FOR ME AND THE LIFE GIVEN TO ME!

**Write Down 5 People You Are Grateful for:**

_____

_____

_____

_____

_____

# Notes

# Notes

# Embrace A Healthy Lifestyle

Everyone knows that it is very important to stay healthy as you age. In order to do this, you must stay active and eat healthy.

There are fun ways to get your exercise in so that you can keep your body, mind and spirit active. There are fun various ways to cook and prepare delicious healthy meals. Embracing a healthy lifestyle is key to being able to grow old gracefully as well as to grow and handle life changes. Remember age is nothing but a number, so no matter what age you are you can follow some of my tips below to live a healthy lifestyle full of life and joy while dwelling in the good things.

## Daily Tips to Staying Active While Embracing a Healthy Lifestyle

1. Walking with a loved one or with a walking group.

2. Stretch daily preferably early mornings.

3. Mild hikes with friends, family and loved ones.

4. YMCA or Community Center Activities.

   - Yoga

   - Exercise and Aerobic Classes

   - Line Dancing Tai Chi

   - Golf Activity Challenge and more...

5. Volunteer.

6. Good Night Sleep.

7. Eating Healthy Nutritious Foods such as:

8. Fruits and Vegetables Whole Foods

9. Herbs and Spices Fresh Juices

10. Cleanse and Detox the Body.

11. Drink at least 8 glasses of water a day.

Eating well along with fitness is the foundation for an overall picture of wellness. Health is Wealth that can make you look and feel fabulous in every aspect of your life.

**Name 3 things you will start to implement into your daily life practice for a healthier you!**

_____

_____

_____

# Notes

# Notes

# Positive Mindset

Having a positive mindset is essential to anyone's growth as well as your dreams and goals. What we think in our minds eventually becomes what we believe. This is why it is so important to speak positive things into our minds and our thoughts about ourselves, many times over each and every day.

**Some of my favorites are:**

I deeply and completely love myself

I Am happy with who I am becoming

I Am strong

I Am a winner

I Am worthy

I Am free to be me

I Am beautiful

I Am enough

There are so many more positive thoughts you can tell yourself everyday throughout the day.

With every negative thought you think, try replacing it with a positive thought repeating the positive thoughts 7 times. With repetition you will learn how to throw negative thoughts out of your mind by replacing them with positive thoughts and this will help you create a positive mindset.

Remember the good book says: For as he thinketh in his heart so is he. Proverbs 23:7

This applies to us women! We want to train our minds to think positive so our hearts can manifest greatness within ourselves.

Defeating negative thoughts will lead to a happier, healthier life of abundance.

Living in a busy society we are constantly going and going but yet not really accomplishing what is most important. Which is pursuing a positive mindset, while reaching you goals and dreams.

Start by transforming your thinking into a positive mindset and you will begin to see things change tremendously toward a happier you!

# Notes

# Notes

# Self-Love And Self-Care

What is self-love and self-care? Well, I'm here to tell you, it is significant in your daily life, happiness, plus your wellbeing.

Let's start with "Self-Love." You must love yourself for who you are. It is inherent in every one of us and very necessary for living a wholesome and fulfilled life.

Living in a world of confusion, often lacking loving role models, healthy relationships and society influences, it comes as no surprise that we implore clarity.

There are some things about us we want to change and find it hard to accept. However, with "Self-Love" you have the power to create the life you want!

I'm going to name a few imperative practices to creating your "Self-Love" such as:

Compassion.

Honor and Appreciate Yourself.

Act on what you need rather than what you want.

Forgive Yourself and Others.

Set Boundaries.

Speak positive words to yourself.

Believe in yourself.

Now let's elaborate on "Self-Care." Some Self-Care practices align from bubble baths to physical exercises. Very few unfortunately dive into the profound meaning of actively engaging in self-care. It's about building a life you don't want to escape from.

Your conscious intentions actively processing personal development and advancement that consist of mental, physical, emotional, social and spiritual growth.

I'm going to name a few pertinent practices to incorporate.

Be creative at doing something that gives you purpose.

Set goals and task to achieve those values.

Commit to yourself at least 30 minutes a few days a week to support your long-term wellness.

Journal about your day. Take a nice candle light bubble bath.

Live in the moment by being mindful throughout the day.

Check in with yourself and your Emotions daily throughout the day.

Write down and choose your action steps going forward from the list of your

"Self-Love" And "Self-Care."

_____

_____

_____

_____

# Notes

# Notes

# Discipline Dedication Determination

These 3 words are what many people run away from.

However, in order to live a life of greatness you must be able to start with these Three D's.

To build on any ideal to the point that you are attaining as well as creating your dreams and goals, there is no easy task. However, it is definitely guaranteed to be worth it all.

*"No one said it was going to be easy".*

Once you start participating in your own personal growth towards your success these Three D's will become more obvious and durable within your success programming.

These tools are extremely powerful and within learning to develop them will have major impact on your success. Everything in life becomes a lot easier once you have developed these tools, in which you will need to use on a regular basis.

Use these Three D's to transform yourself and to accomplish your dreams and goals, while shifting your life to a better and greater you!

# Notes

_____

_____

_____

_____

_____

_____

_____

_____

_____

_____

_____

_____

_____

_____

_____

_____

_____

# Notes

# Patience Is Power

Patience is an emotional free practice of watching and knowing when to make a move. You will also want to gain an understanding of how to transform irritation and frustration with patience. If you want success in your life you must understand that patience is power.

For example, if you want to plant a tree you must allow time for that tree to grow. Meanwhile during the growth of any tree, goals and dreams, it will require your patience for all of them to sprout. Anything you want to accomplish in life worthwhile will take patience. Just like a tree, patience can be associated and affiliated within many aspects of life. However, the key here is to master, grasp and develop the art of patience that will circulate your power as you are working on yourself.

A lot of times we will allow the impatient self to take over and by doing so we may fall short on our goal achievements. Exercising patience does not mean never protesting or giving up, but only ever doing so in a considered fashion: never impetuously, never prettily and never pointlessly.

Understand that patience is power. Take your time as well as be mindful by taking one step at a time.

**Name 2 goals:**

_____

_____

**Write down how you will take action daily exercising your "Power of Patience"**

_____

_____

_____

_____

Philippians 4:6

_"Do not be anxious about anything, but in everything by prayer and supplication with thanksgiving let your requests be made known to God"_

# Notes

# Notes

# Meditation

Meditation is an uncomplicated practice available to all, which can reduce stress and anxiety. It can also increase calmness, a sense of peace and promote positivity as well as happiness.

Learning how is straight forward, the benefits are instant. It's a practice of mindfulness in which you are paying attention to the breath as it goes in and out, with stillness. A process in which we shift from thinking to feeling, which allows the complexity of the mind and leads to the simplicity of the heart.

Incorporating meditation into your daily practice before starting your day can help create a positive and productive mindset throughout your day. Tuning into your breath and body first thing in the morning, you become more aware of your thoughts and that "out of control" mind. Some thoughts make sense although, some seem to derive out of nowhere. Through regular practice you can gain control of your thoughts, which is learning how to master yourself and way of thinking.

# Notes

# Notes

# Become What You Believe

Ask yourself "What do you believe about yourself". Your very being and existence of your life is a reflection on what you think and believe about you. We actually create our own reality. We must be willing to do the work and it's going to take work, hard work! Success for yourself, goals, dreams as well as any accomplishments worthwhile just does not happen and appear out of nowhere. There is a process. You must make it happen through your actions and your thoughts. It's all in the baby steps, not expecting it to happen overnight.

Also surround yourself with likeminded people on the same victorious path. It's never too late to execute what you believe. In life it's all about growing and learning to trust yourself. Creating a better and greater version of you all the way to the end. Never stopping or giving up, realizing that you have the power. Don't allow living in nostalgia prevent you from moving forward at being your best self. Let go, pray, have faith and trust the journey. The past does not define you, live the life you were meant to live. "Do unto others as you would have them do unto you."

The Law of Attraction.

What you put out is what you get back.

**Write down 5 things you believe about yourself**

_____

_____

_____

_____

_____

**Write down 5 things that will start the process of "Becoming What You Believe"**

_____

_____

_____

_____

_____

When You Know Better You Do Better!

# Notes

# Notes

# Forgive And Grow

Forgive yourself and forgive others. This is one of the most important factors of ones growth. Accepting what has happened in the past however, it doesn't have to be okay. Remember I mentioned in the previous chapter, we must let go so the past does not hold us prisoner, such as grudges, failures etc? By letting go, we will be happier and not give the past hurts, people and pain any power.

We need all our power to manifest and stay focused on the present.

We also want to forgive ourselves. I know a lot of us have put ourselves through much self-destruction but, we must forgive in order to move forward. We created our own suffering situations within our lives that we knew at the time was not good or right for us. However, we made a choice to change and now it's time to stand in the mirror and humbly say 7 times or more to ourselves "I Forgive You!"

Forgiveness is such an important tool in our constant growth in life. When we forgive, we let go and when we let go we generate space for more wonderful, positive and new experiences in life. We create peace!

One of the greatest gifts this life has to offer!

**Write down 7 things you need to let go in order to:**

**"Forgive and Grow"**

_____

_____

_____

_____

_____

_____

Luke 6:37

*Judge not, and ye shall not be judged: condemn not, and ye shall not be condemned: forgive, and ye shall be forgiven.*

# Notes

# Notes

# You Gotta Have Faith

Faith brings the utmost peace, love, understanding, compassion, prosperity and healing. With having faith you must have a relationship with your "Higher Power", whomever or whatever that may be for you.

It's all in believing that someone or something deserves to be trusted. Your dreams, your goals and your journey, needs to be trusted with hope that they're deserving to becoming your reality.

Through your most difficult moments and time faith is the decision to love, no matter the circumstances. It's easy to lose hope in a world full of poverty and pain as love can seem pointless. However, it's our greatest purpose that will keep hope alive, even when it seems impossible.

Pray and ask God, the universe or whatever higher power you believe in, for the strength you need to love and guide you through your most difficult time.

I will share a few of my favorite scriptures to embody into your daily lifestyle.

Romans 10:17

*Faith comes by hearing and hearing by the word of God.*

Proverbs 3:5-6

*Trust in the Lord with all your heart; and lean not unto your own understanding. In all thy ways acknowledge him, and he shall direct thy paths.*

Mathew 7: 7-8

*Ask, and it shall be given you; seek, and ye shall find; knock, and it shall be opened unto you: For every one that ask receiveth; and he that seeketh findeth; and to Him that knocked it shall be opened.*

Surround yourself with people you admire, so you can walk along the same path.

Help others, sometimes the greatest strength and joy comes through helping others in need.

Choose a hobby and a source of inspiration to help you get through faith by inspiring books, self-empowerment videos, motivational speakers, music and more.

# Notes

# Notes

# Get Out of the Comfort Zone

It is so easy to stay within the boundaries of what is comfortable, than to face the unknown. However, to go beyond and reach the impossible that is possible for your dreams and goals we must step out of our comfort zone and feel everything and rise, which means we must venture out to face fear!

When we limit ourselves to what we already know, it's likely that you are missing out on professional opportunities, life experiences, personal growth and more.

Getting out of our safe cocoon will allow us to live fearlessly, bold and courageous. These are the tools we need to pursue our purpose with firm faith and belief in ourselves.

It's innate to want to stick with things to which we're accustomed. But the more time we spend in this zone, the more difficult it will be to break free from that space. Many people spend their entire lives there, never sacrificing the potential for much better possibilities.

Gradually push yourself to take on bigger (strategic) risks. Challenge your weakness by stretching yourself little by little.

Here are five reasons why you need to get out of your comfort zone

1. It Builds Confidence.

2. Develops Inner Strength.

3. Creates A Purpose In Your Life.

4. You'll Become More Creative.

5. You Won't Know What Could Have Been.

**A few tools to overcome fear and breakout of your comfort zone:**

1. Move Towards Your Fears.

2. Change Your Routine.

3. Let Go Of Control.

4. Try Something New Until It Feels Comfortable.

5. Do Something You Wouldn't Normally Consider.

6. Write A List of Growth Goals.

7. Do A Live Social Media Video.

**Write Down 5 Action Steps You Will Implement To Get Out Of Your Comfort Zone Today.**

_____

_____

_____

_____

_____

Philippians 4:13

*I can do all things through Christ who strengthens me.*

# Notes

# Notes

# You Got This

You can do anything you put your mind to. Whatever it is you want to do in life, you can do it.

If it's losing the weight you desire, you got this.

Owning your own business at 50+, that you've always seen yourself doing, you got this.

Running that marathon at age 80, you got this. Being physically fit and in shape, you got this. Creating a legacy for your family, you got this.

Living a life of financial freedom full of luxury and abundance, you got this.

Go ahead and break out into your fearless, bold, courageous, self-improved you. No one can do it but you!

Knowing that you believe you can will help you succeed and get whatever your heart desires.

**YOU GOT THIS!**

# Notes

# Notes

# Encouragement

We all need support, confidence, hope in our lives. I encourage you today, to pursue your dreams and goals that will bring you joy, peace, abundance, wealth, health and success.

Try to stimulate the development of what you do by having a positive mindset, believing in yourself and showing up for yourself.

The Great Muhammad Ali said: "The fight is won or lost far away from witnesses. Behind the lines, in the gym and out there on the road, long before I dance under those lights."

Begin your day with encouraging quotes, self- empowerment books, devotion, etc. No matter what you're going through, you have the power and the strength to overcome all obstacles.

*"Your past does not define you! Your future is currently waiting for you. The present is yours to uphold & live in the now!"*

~ Ms. Diamond

*"Believe you can and you're halfway there."*

~ Theodore Roosevelt

# Notes

# Notes

# You Have Everything You Need

Once you realize that you have the breath that God gave you to breathe and your health, there's hope and if you have hope, you have everything!

When you look inside yourself, your talents, skills, gifts etc. and begin to nourish, polish and elevate these qualities, you will recognize that you have everything you need to flourish your dreams and goals.

Along with everything that we have, we will also need to work on ourselves from the inside to elevate our gifted blessings to manifest into reality.

Beginning with a vision. Without a vision you will be all over the place with no direction. Realize where you are going. Nothing starts without a dream.

Have an innate belief in yourself. You must believe in you and see yourself as living your dream life now.

Keep striving and keep it moving forward. Remember it's hard to beat a person who never gives up!

All that is required is the ability, confidence, fearlessness, courage, bravery and boldness in one's ability to get your own needs met.

Be willing to put in the work. Work on you and your dreams and goals because they are possible. Hard work is essential to a successful and achievable lifestyle.

Commitment and perseverance are significant key tools that will help you put into action everything you already have inside of you. It's just waiting for you to crack the shell and open.

If you could understand that you already have everything you need, you'd stop wasting your time and procrastinating. Take control of your mindset, have some heart and just be you!

A lot of times we think and feel that we're not enough. When in fact that is far from the truth. We may feel like we need to be more before we can become our greatest version of ourselves. However, if you can accept that you're already enough, then you'll have what you need to succeed.

**You Are Enough! You Got This!**

Write Down Your Talents, Skills, Gifts Etc.

_____

_____

_____

_____

_____

NOW PUT THEM INTO ACTION AND MAKE IT HAPPEN!

DEMONSTRATION IS MANIFESTATION

# Notes

# Notes

# Praying Is Powerful

There is incredible power and potential in prayer.

Praying in powerful!

Praying to our higher power, the God of the Universe is important to our everyday lifestyle. I believe prayer changes things. Miracles are created and opportunities are given. We have the connection to reach our full potential.

As you go forth and grow to your dreams and goals, pray and watch endless activities just happen for you. Prayer will lead and guide you in the direction and journey you are seeking.

We aren't perfect but as we grow and take steps forward, we become more alive and more engaged with the plan God has in place.

Pray everyday as well as through the day and watch the impact of Gods transformation for our lives do incredible work. Through prayer we can conquer the impossible. God moves mountains and he will do the same for you.

Watch Him Work For You!

# Notes

# Notes

# Get Ready to Blow Your Mind

This is your time. Life is on your side. Whatever it is you desire to do, you and only you can make it happen.

We cannot afford to live in fear anymore. Be willing to take the chances in your life so much, that you'll be proud of who you have become.

Take your fear and turn it into fearlessness. God has you in the palm of his right hand. That means you are covered and protected by Him at all times. Trust his process for you as you go forth with your dreams and goals.

Miracles start to happen when you give as much energy to your Dreams and Goals as you do to your Fears!!!

Ask and it shall be given you; see and you will find; Knock and the door will be open to you! Matthew 7:7

You are capable of amazing things. Know that if He brings you to it; He will bring you through it.

Dream Big! Work Hard!

Get Ready to Blow Your Mind!!!

# Notes

# Notes

# About the Author

As a young girl, not knowing her biological family and adopted at the age of 5. I Began to live a life away from home at the young age of 13. If I can do it you can too. No one said it was going to be easy. However, we are all born winners and we all were born with a purpose. Go deep inside yourself with prayer, faith and meditation to help find your purpose. Live the life you were born to live. A Life of abundance, it's your birthright!

This book will help guide you and begin the process of making your dreams and goals a reality. Never give up no matter what struggles you may encounter. Be willing to defy the odds, believe in you and make it happen. Sending you lots of love and positive vibes as you conquer your freedom to do you and be you! Keep Your Head Up! Peace and Blessings!

www.ingramcontent.com/pod-product-compliance
Lightning Source LLC
Chambersburg PA
CBHW072209090426
42740CB00012B/2452